The People's Voice
Former Arizona Sheriff Richard Mack

This information is offered for educational purposes only; not to be taken as legal advice.

MAINE-PATRIOT.com
3 Linnell Circle
Brunswick, Maine 04011

maine-patriot.com

Hope Deferred

The Sheriff is "the ultimate authority in the land"

The People's Voice
Former Arizona Sheriff Richard Mack

Contents

Hope Deferred

Richard Mack

Born Richard Ivan Mack,1952

Richard Ivan Mack, popularly known as **Sheriff Mack**, is a former sheriff of Graham County, Arizona and Libertarian candidate for United States Senate election in Arizona, 2006.

He is also a member of the Oath Keepers.

Mack has authored books relating to gun ownership and the role that law enforcement should, in his opinion, play in America. He currently speaks at seminars on constitutional issues relating to gun control, law enforcement, States' rights, the Oath of Office, and the farce otherwise known as the drug war.

Mack received national attention in *Mack v. United States* (later restyled to *Printz v. United States*) in his tenure as a local sheriff, for opposition to the Brady Handgun Violence Prevention Act, on the basis that it is unconstitutional due to congressional action to compel state officers to execute Federal law.

In 2009, Richard Mack appeared in television interviews where he discussed his membership in Oath Keepers, and the importance of the police and military in upholding their oaths to the United States Constitution.

http://www.sheriffmack.com/

Hope Deferred

Power of the County Sheriff

My name is Richard Mack and I'm the former Sheriff of Grand City, Arizona.

• The Sheriff is "the ultimate authority in the land."

The Sheriff is the only elected law enforcement officer in the United States - and therefore in his County. He's the only official who reports directly to the Source of power. He reports directly to "we the people" on the land.

He is sovereign in this regard because he reports directly to the Sovereigns. That is why the Sheriff is the ultimate authority on the land. He's not a bureaucrat from Washington, DC.

The President of the United States cannot tell your Sheriff what to do. So certainly, none of the other auxiliary departments underneath the president can tell the Sheriff what to do, and that includes the IRS, the EPA, OSHA, the FBI, the DEA, none of those agencies can tell the Sheriff what to do.

But when they are in his sovereign jurisdiction, *he* can tell *them* what to do.

Ingratitude, Disdain   9

• The Oath

It's really alarming how many peace officers, police-men, law enforcement officers, Sheriffs, and Chiefs of Police — who have actually taken an Oath of Office to uphold and defend, protect and preserve, the United States Constitution — and then when you present them with that clause or idea, that that's exactly what they should be doing, they claim that it isn't their job to uphold and defend the Constitution — that which they have already sworn an oath to do!

So that's what I find really disturbing. But I think it's the evolution that's taken effect in our country today. Also it's a result, or a consequence, or a branch, of what is wrong in America.

America is off track. We have replaced our Constitution, which was the bulwark of our freedom in this country, with political agendas, political selfishness — and ultimately, political correctness has replaced our Constitution.

And so is it any wonder that we are so far off track. And my message is that law enforcement owns part of that problem. And we need to correct it.

• The Government, the Sheriff, the Constitution

Now, the government and the Sheriff are pretty much equal. The government is the sovereign leader over the state. The Sheriff could probably supercede the government within his county, because he is the ultimate protector of the people within his jurisdiction.

He can't let anybody violate the Constitution in his

county.

He cannot allow anyone to violate the rights of the people within his jurisdiction. It doesn't matter if it's the governor, or the president, the IRS, or the FBI, — he's in charge of protecting the constitutional freedoms of his jurisdiction.

The governor, yes, oversees the state, and he or she is very powerful. And they are equal in some ways, and have the same responsibility to the people who elected them, and that is, to hold and defend the Constitution.

• State Sovereignty and The Federal Law

I was probably the first Sheriff in the United States to sue the Federal Government for doing that very thing, for promulgating a bill or law, or statute, that directly commandeers the Sheriff for federal building. As I look back, I'm really grateful that we won a case in the United States Supreme Court, and I have yet to see throughout American history if there's been another case with the Supreme Court, won by a Sheriff — a sitting Sheriff.

Sheriff Prince and I ended up taking this case all the way to the Supreme Court. We won in this very issue of state sovereignty — local autonomy — and the power of the county.

For when other legislative bodies pass a supposed law that forces the Sheriff to violate his Oath of Office to protect and defend the Constitution, what does he do?

And Judge Roll, in my case, actually said that Sheriff Mack is thus forced to choose between keeping his oath, or obeying the Act. And I think he nailed it right on the head there. That's the key question. What does all of law enforcement, and what do all the Sheriff's across the country do when a statute forces them to violate their constitutional oath?

Well, I think it's easy. You keep your word to your oath. That's the ultimate law. The supreme law of the land is the Constitution. Nothing supersedes the Constitution, so let's put it back in its proper place.

And I would say, there was a Sheriff from Montana who did not join the law suit, who I agree with. He did it the right way — he just said "NO! we're not doing the Brady Bill in this county. And I believe that was Sheriff Nixon. And as I look back, I wish that that was what we had done.

• Just Say "NO!" and send it back to Washington

After looking back at my lawsuit and the subsequent victory in the United States Supreme Court, then I wish the Sheriffs in Arizona had simply all signed a letter, initially, and sent it back to Washington, DC, to the White House, and CC'd it over to the Congress and the Justice Department, letting them know that "We're not doing the Brady Bill in Arizona, and thank you very much for your efforts, but it won't be applied here.

• "Federal Agents Need Permission." Castenada vs. Big Horn County.

Yeah, that was a very powerful case, disavowed by the judge in the case, by the way, but it was a requirement of the settlement in the case, that Sheriff Madus devise a way to make sure that the Federal Government couldn't come in and do what they did to the Castenada family, trying to arrest them — well, they *did* arrest them — at 1:00 o'clock in the morning — for being illegal immigrants.

And, of course, nobody's trying to do that now when we have them all over the place. The thing of it was... the Castenada's required that as part of the settlement.

And Dave Madus actually came up with the idea. And they were obeying it. The Federal Government was obeying it. And other counties in Wyoming practiced the same policy. It wasn't a law, but it was a policy established through a court order. Of a court settlement — I should say.

I don't believe they're doing it too much, now. So we've got a lot of work to do.

• Key people in local government to support the Sheriff — County Commissioners, County Attorney

The first thing I would like to see would be the County Commissioners... The County Commissioners should support their Sheriffs with proper legislation or resolutions to have him enforce the Constitution.

So, if they pass a law saying, say, the Federal Government have this HR45 that Barack Obama is trying to shove down our throats, right now, to have a national registry for firearms and firearm owners in their County, and to have a national licensure granted from Washington, DC, to keep and bear arms. Which is already guaranteed in the 2nd Amendment. Let's say that that's really going to be pushed, and then the Federal Government is going to come out and perhaps confiscate weapons and/or ammunitions... What does the local authority do?

Well the County Commissioners should pass a Resolution saying that there will be no more federal gun control in this County, and the Sheriff endorse it. So when the FEDS come in, the Sheriff stands.

He shouldn't need that Resolution, but it would be nice to have it, because the 2nd Amendment is there and it's already sworn — we're back to that again — he's already sworn to support and defend the Constitution and the Bill of Rights of which the 2nd Amendment is a part — a key integral part of freedom as established by our Founding Fathers.

And why was the 2nd Amendment put there in the first place? Well that's what we all need to understand — the intent of the Founding Fathers on the 2nd Amendment.

. . . so that the people of this country would have the final say in controlling their Government. The ultimate power of the 2nd Amendment is so that the people remain in charge, to be able to fight off elusive Government. That's why the 2nd Amendment is there.

And the other one that really needs to back the Sheriff in what's going on, is the county attorney.

It's not essential to have those others — the Sheriff can do it on his own, he doesn't need to ask permission of anybody in the county, or across the country — he doesn't need to ask the Barber down on Main Street, or anyone else how he's going to keep his Oath of Office.

He's bound by his word, and he's also bound by the Constitution.

• Department of Homeland Security

The Department of Homeland Security should have absolutely nothing to do with your Sheriff's office. Let me say that again. Absolutely Nothing! OK?

Homeland Security has only been around for a few years, since 9/11 of course, and right now we have Janet Napolitano, who used to be the Governor of Arizona, saying that Veterans and people who believe in Ron Paul, and people who believe in the Constitution, and people who believe in the Bible, and who believe in gun rights, are all dangerous, and pose some sort of danger to the Federal Government.

Well, I guess she might be right, if the government is out of control, and tyrannical and abusive. Then, yeah, she ought to be worried, but otherwise those people in those events are extremely peaceful.

And she even mentioned the Libertarians, even though all Libertarians have to swear an oath of non-aggression and non-violence. So how do they make that list?

• DHS and Federal Funding

The Sheriff shouldn't be taking money from the FEDS in the first place, and then they don't have to worry about that. And all of the states should wake the heck up, and I really do mean wake up the heck up!

If they would stop sending our money to Washington, DC, then Washington, DC, wouldn't have our money to hold over us anymore. So maybe it's all too simple. But the Federal Government doesn't create money — they take money.

And they take money from the states, and from the people. So why do the states sit here and worry about every $10 dollars they send to Washington, DC. — that they only get $1 dollar back. Well, keep your $10 dollars and you won't have to worry about any of that.

• Citizen Support — Militia/Posse

Well the citizens are the boss of the Sheriff, and so they need to let the Sheriff know what they want him to do. But if 99.9% of the people in his county asked him to violate the Constitution, he couldn't do it, no matter what. He has to keep his word.

This is not a Democracy, in a Democracy that would be OK — the rule of the majority would win out — that's the Democracy.

In a Constitutional Republic the rights of the individual — even if it's just one person in his county, must be protected. And so the people from - Oh - the "M" word — the Militia — the Posse.

If you look up the word, Militia in the dictionary, or Google the definition of Militia, it's the same thing as the local Posse, which the Sheriff has the power to call out, and actually order the people to help him in the execution of the law in keeping the peace. And that's where the people will really come out.

• *"The County Sheriff: America's Last Hope"* by Richard Mack. Buy it today!

How can citizens support their Sheriff? Well, he works for you. You've gotta read this, and take it to him, and say, you know what? There was a Sheriff who sued the Federal Government and won a case, in the issue of State's Rights. We'd like you to consider this.

And it's only 50 pages, so he can read this while he eats a donut. <Big Smile> Hey, I was in law enforcement for 20 years, I know . . .

• The MIAC report (DHS) targets Veterans, Libertarians, Ron Paul supporters, 9/11 Truthers, etc.

The MIAC report was absolutely absurd. Anyone thinking that that is OK has got a screw loose somewhere, and they call *us* crazy? We mean no harm to any individual on the face of the planet. This is a peaceful movement. This as a movement to resolve our Constitution — Yes, — and we will stand fast in that — and we're not going to move backward for anybody.

But we mean no harm to anyone else. We don't want to hurt anybody. We certainly don't want a fight or a war, or anything of that nature.

But we're not giving up our guns. We're not giving up our ammunition. And we're not giving up our children.

We're not giving up our religion. And we're certainly not going to be giving up any more of our liberty and freedom.

And if you'll really study what's going on in our country, you would come face to face with the conclusion that I also have in the Book — the best book on the planet right now about freedom — that every citizen in this country should read — the bottom line of this whole book is that it presents this thesis of the book — that the greatest threat to constitutional God Given American liberty *is our own Federal Government!!!*

• **Corruption and Recall**

The worst thing that can happen in this country is for a county Sheriff to be corrupt. They really have to be removed. And because he is corrupt, he has a lot of people in his pocket, or he's in the pockets of other people. I don't think that happens an awful lot, but I know for a fact that this happens and is happening now. So some states don't even have recall laws.

The only way he can be removed in some states is if you convict him of a felony. Well, that's happened a few times. There are local laws, and I suggest that people use them. Or, you find a place to live where the Sheriff is honest and keeps his Oath of Office.

But to the Sheriffs who are corrupt, luckily it's a small percentage, we want... we need all Sheriff's to come to the realization that the Oath of Office is their ultimate goal and purpose and duty, and if you're just going to take the oath as a ceremony to get your picture in the papers at the beginning of your term, then you've violated the Constitution and you've violated the trust of the people.

A recall is just a signature drive where people in the county sign a petition to have another election, and the Sheriff is still on that ballot, or another corrupt elected official. He's still on that ballot, but it puts him up for another election and it gives the people another chance to kick him out.

• Real ID Act and Gun Control

The Real ID Act is one of many coming down the pike in Washington, DC. Let's go back to the 2nd Amendment. What the 2nd Amendment does, without question — it would take any high school student maybe 5 minutes to find the intent of the Founding Fathers — they would have to go try to find it, because they're not taught the 2nd Amendment and the intent of the Founding Fathers in schools.

I've been a government teacher in High School before and I know, it does not teach the truth. Most of the government books in this country's school system do not teach the truth about our foundation, or about our government, or about the Founding Fathers.

But there's a lot of information out there, you can find it, but the Federal Government is trying to force more gun control down our throats, they are trying to force this government down our throat, that's also going to have a part to play about gun control, and I simply don't trust any of it.

But the overall socialistic agenda that is saturating Washington, DC politics right now. It's all unconstitutional. Our government is not here to feed us, to clothe us, to take care of us, to educate us, to basically take care of us.

And let me warn you, friends, if you want the Federal Government to take care of you, they will! And that should scare you to death.

But the National ID Act, and all that stuff, HR45, the bottom line is that there's already about 22,000 gun control laws in this country, all of which are unconstitutional, every one of them.

The people have the right to keep and bear arms; but what gun I own, and how I get it, and how much ammo I have, and how many guns I have, guess what — I don't want to be rude here — but it's none of your business! And it's certainly none of my government's business.

• Stopping the Real ID Act

The Sheriff can refuse any order or policy, or suggestion, or law, or anything else from Washington, DC, or from the State Capital if it violates the rights of the people. The Sheriff is the ultimate check and balance. And he usually has a gun.

• Free Speech and the Media

Freedom of the press, freedom of speech, it's all combined together, and a lot of times these same groups that are being attacked, are the ones who are the most vocal. So that's why Janet Napolitano is coming after them, because they have to label you with something, so people won't listen to you.

So who jumps on board on that attack? Well, it's usually ABC, CBS and NBC, and CNN, what are these? Government media outlets?

The reason why we have freedom of the press is not so we can read about LaBraun James and the sports page of the newspapers, it's so that the press is actually a check and balance against overzealous government, so that the people will always hear the truth about what's really going on.

Well that's not happening anymore.

• Water Rights and States Rights - the Wet Lands Act back in the 90's

There was a big rain in somebody's ranch and it formed a little pond on it, and the government came in and took over this guys land because there was a pond on it, and there's been so many ridiculous things lately.

The Endangered Species Act has a lot of stupidity in it from Washington, DC.

The EPA has done a lot of stupid things in the name of supposedly protecting our environment. Cost a lot of jobs. If you want to see there, most jobs have been lost in this country in the last 20 years, put it right at the doorstep of the EPA.

The Wet Lands Act, and now they think they own all the water. Governor Simington back in the 90's also showed the Federal Government where they couldn't balance the budget, and there was no budget for awhile when Bill Clinton was in office.

Governor Simington said, fine, we don't need you guys. We'll run our own Grand Canyon — it's ours anyway. We don't need you guys running our Grand Canyon.

Well, its the same principle. The Governors of every individual state, and then the counties and Boards of

Commissioners, and Boards of Supervisors need to let the Federal Government know — you don't own the water in this state! This is a sovereign state. We are in charge within the borders of this state. We are in charge, not you!!!

The states created you. You don't supercede the creator. The Federal Government didn't even exist when we started the Revolutionary War. It was formed afterwards. So when we fought for freedom it was for state sovereignty — not for a strong central government. One place where Alexander Hamilton was wrong.

• The 10th Amendment

The 10th Amendment is the basis of my lawsuit. The 10th Amendment is where it guarantees the power of the sovereign to the states or to the people. Which shows the power of the people here.

And to paraphrase the 10th Amendment — this is really what the 10th Amendment says — It's the Founding Fathers telling all future generations of government, especially in Washington, DC, that just in case you really want to get creative, or if you think we forgot something, you can't do that either.

That's the 10th Amendment.

• The Purpose of Government

Usually, you can be certain that if Washington, DC passes another law, it's going to cost taxes and jobs. And then they'll turn around and create a welfare state for those people to collect more benefits and entitlements.

It's absolutely amazing that the Icon of the Democratic Party was JFK, and he said, "Ask not what your country can do for you, but what you can do for your country." Anybody remember that principle?

Show me a Democrat, anywhere in government, and a Republican, for that matter, in Washington, DC, who believes that principle.

Government is not here to take care of us. Government is here to protect our borders. Huh? They've done a bang up job there? But No – It's so opposite of what it was intended to be that it's absolutely scary.

• Thr Duty of the Sheriff and Health Freedom

Well, first of all the county Sheriff has the duty of protecting the businesses that are offering alternative health care to citizens. Those businesses have a right to exist. Let me say, for the record, make this your club.

I use'em. Right now if you looked at the evidence, doctors kill by making mistakes on prescriptions, and other mistakes, about 125,000 deaths per year.

Guns supposedly are only about 20,000 such deaths. Why aren't we registering and going after doctors?

We've actually strengthened the FDA and given the FDA more power, and they don't have any power to begin with, but they keep stealing and usurping it.

But they're actually going after some of those herbal companies, or whole food companies. Most of these supposedly herbal medications are simply whole foods. They're just concentrated, and I use them all the time.

And so does my wife and family. And we will continue to do so. And for anybody to say that these companies should be shut down so that we could have more chemotherapy and more drugs shoved down our throats, like Prozac and Zolof, and all those other things that are destroying our children, is ridiculous.

• The Sheriff reports to the People

The Sheriff is not a puppet for the Courts or for the Legislators. He's his own boss, again. Who does he report to? He reports to the people. And he has to weigh that, above all other elected or appointed public officials who are going after a citizen in this country.

It doesn't matter if it's the IRS, or a judge, or whatever. The judge cannot expect, and should not expect the Sheriff to go along with an unconstitutional order. In fact, no one, not the nations, or law enforcement, can be held accountable for disobeying an unlawful order.

• Oath Keepers

Oath Keepers! Oath Keepers has been around for about 2 or 3 months, and I got to know Steve Freeman and Stuart Rose with Oathkeepers, and the relationship that we have is an obvious one, and an easy one. I've been preaching about the Oath of Office for about 20 years, and now they've made it a national campaign.

And I'll tell you what, when I was in Lexington at the Oath Ceremony, where there was a crowd of about 400 citizens, law enforcement, retired military, all of us joining together, raising our arms and taking an Oath, or taking, or reaffirming our Oath to uphold and defend the

United States Constitution, I'll tell you what, it brought forth a tear to my eyes. It was one of the most powerful moments I've ever participated in.

• Blackwater

You know, you can't contract out what the Army is supposed to do, and what they're contractually supposed to be doing to protect, and then kind of give cart blanch to a private company to do that which the military is supposed to be doing, you know, that really puts the government and the military in a precarious position.

And we have seen what happens when you do that. Who do these people — a private company — who do they report to? Who's their boss? If they violate the contract, who's responsible, the government, or that company? Do we get mad at them? What do we do with them? Fire them? Stop their contract? Take the money back? Sue 'em? All that stuff is not part of a military operation.

• Private Armed Security

Something with Andrews International, or anybody else. They can work for private companies, and they shouldn't be hired by the government. They're a private company. Their allegiance is not to the American people or to the Constitution. Their allegiance is to make money. They're a private company.

And I don't mind a private company making money, I fully support the capitalist society that we're supposed to have. Capitalism works a lot better than Socialism or Communism.

• Martial Law

I think that the ultimate protection that the Sheriff will give his people is from other government agencies that want to run roughshod over his people and his County.

We saw what happened in Waco when Sheriffs stand back and trust the Federal Government. The Federal Government doesn't have a very good track record. So the last thing you want to do is trust government.

And in fact, Patrick Henry warned us that we should never trust government officials, but shackle them down with parameters and the chains of the Constitution, like he said.

And Thomas Jefferson said that the price of freedom is eternal vigilance.

The ones who are supposed to be careful, are all of us, we the people, it's our government, it's what we do. This is us. So we have really got to be careful.

The Sheriff is the ultimate protector, again. To protect us from all enemies, both foreign and domestic.

It doesn't matter where they come from. Whether they come from Washington, DC, or the State House, or where ever else .

So our Martial Law, and it's this, the Sheriff, if he's organized enough, and has his Posse ready to go, his armed Posse ready to go anywhere in his County or this Country, then FEMA, and those from the Federal Government who want to institute Martial Law, they can tell 'em to go somewhere else.

There's not going to be enough manpower to do all this anyway. If they want to do Martial Law from Honolulu Hawaii to Bangor Maine, there's absolutely not enough manpower. It has to be local people.

So the Sheriffs are going to be asked to be part of the Martial Law. The Sheriff can say, no thanks, go somewhere else. We don't need you here. We've got it under control. The Sheriffs really are going to have to exercise some real leadership and planning on that one.

• Building a Militia/Posse

Sheriff Joe Pike from Phoenix Arizona has already set that example for all of us. On the last count, I think he has about 5,000 on his Posse. When I was Sheriff I had about 125.

Our Search and Rescue, our entire team was all Posse members — all volunteers. And they were excellent. We can exercise... The Sheriff can exercise his authority, to call on volunteers, however he wants, and he can spare the citizens a lot of money in doing so.

• Foreign Troops — The United Nations

United Nations troops being in the United States even for a little exercise — even for *any* exercise is something we should all be very concerned about. We had 'em back in Arizona, when I was Sheriff.

They weren't in my county. They were in a neighboring county. We got pictures of them and asked why they were there, and they said that they were there on a "peace-keeping" mission.

Well, I thought we were already at peace in Arizona and in the United States. Why do we need the United Nations?

Let me tell you right now, this mentality and the propaganda that's going around that the counties are subject to the state legislature, and that the state legislature is coupled to the Federal Government, and that the Federal Government is subjected somehow to this international government called the United Nations.

That is absolutely atrocious, it's stupid. It's not the truth. It's not free. The United Nations has no authority over the United States, It has no authority over you, unless you give it to them.

And the first thing we need to do is get our country's sovereignty back and kick the United Nations out or dissolve it.

And we shouldn't be in the United Nations.

The United Nations was first propagandized as a means for keeping the peace throughout the world, and since they've been there, there's been more poverty, which they said they were gonna stop, which is absurd, but there's been more wars under the tutelage of the United Nations than any other time in the history of the world.

• FEMA and Katrina

I think the bottom line of FEMA, during Katrina, is a typical example of what you get when you turn things over to Washington, DC,

New Orleans and the State of Louisiana should have

been prepared, and should not have depended on FEMA to do anything.

But they did, and they all paid for it dearly. And we're in a dire situation if we think that FEMA's going to take care of us in this effort.

They don't have a good track record. Man, here's another bureaucracy of Washington, DC, that doesn't have a good track record. The IRS doesn't have one, the FBI doesn't have one, it just goes on and on and on folks. So, I think the warning from Ronald Reagan when he said that government isn't the solution to the problem, government IS the problem, was so true, and we need to wake up to that fact.

• The IRS

Well, the IRS had a hearing before Congress in 1998 where General Laird and Jennifer Long and other employees who were current agents of the IRS testified that the IRS routinely fabricate evidence against citizens who they know couldn't adequately defend themselves. Who couldn't afford financially to defend themselves against the IRS, so the end result is, through this criminal act, that people would just pay the money. And so what happened to the IRS, after that?

After solid proof was given to Congress, who is supposed to oversee the IRS, what did the IRS do? Did they investigate? Did they fire anybody? Did they put anybody in jail for all of these illegal and criminal acts? No! Congress said that we want the IRS offices open on Saturdays and we want the IRS to be more user friendly.

That's like telling the Mafia to be more user friendly, except the Mafia has a bit more scruples than the IRS.

• The EPA

Well the EPA is mentioned in my case on page 15 and if you read *Mack vs. United States,* **the EPA was ruled to be unconstitutional in the 1970's** and yet, they've gotten more power since that ruling. And I think that's a typical example, just like in my case, *Mack vs. United States,* that ruling has been ignored.

And it says that **state legislatures are not subject to federal direction,** and that the states and the counties, and local jurisdictions actually standing up to the Federal Government and preventing incursions form the Federal Government are one of the Constitution's **"structural protections of liberty."**

And its all right there in the case. So, the Federal Government doesn't have authority over us unless we give it to them.

• The Federal Reserve System

The Federal Reserve System is probably the biggest mistake that our county has made, along with the IRS, but they go together hand in hand, they're one and the same, but the Federal Reserve isn't federal, It's owned by private banks.

There's no questions that the Federal Reserve is owned by private banks. It's not federal. So how did we do that? Congress, you've got a lot of work to do, and yet, out representatives in Washington, DC, pretend that it has something to do with the government, and that it's all proper. **But it is not!!!**

• 9/11

Well, I've been asked about 9/11 a lot, of the bombing of the World Trade Center and the Pentagon,

What happened, then, was certainly a national disaster, and a catastrophe, and I hated watching that.

I mean, it tore my heart out. The bottom-line is, I'm not gonna say that I know what happened, because I don't, but what I do know is that the report from the Federal Government is not true. And I want, more than anything... I want to call right now for an independent investigation so that we can get to the bottom of it.

Have another government investigation of it — an independent investigation of what happened on September 11, 2001. **And I'm volunteering to be part of that.**

• Hemp and Medical Marijuana

Hemp has about 2,000 domestic uses. From oil and paper, to fuel — make fuel out of hemp. Hemp was made illegal when they made Marijuana illegal.

Hemp has no THC in it. It's not a narcotic, and it could literally save the economy of this country. And if government officials are so concerned about global warming, then why not harvest hemp?

Hemp could solve half or the world's problems that they're crying about all the time. Plus the medical use of Marijuana is something that absolutely should be explored.

And for everybody to say in government, and police alike, that people just want to smoke Marijuana because it's fun or they want to get high on it.

I know people about whom that absolutely is not true, and if somebody is dying, what do you care if they smoke Marijuana? It's not going to hurt you, and if it makes them feel better, more power to it.

And there's one thing that the Democrats and Republican seemingly have not understood, and that is, why don't you just let people alone, and let them live and let live.

• War on Drugs

I don't support any of that. I don't support the Drug War. After I served as an undercover narcotics officer, I started questioning the Drug War, and right after the IRS, the War on Drugs is the 2nd biggest farce this country has ever come up with.

• Ron Paul

I agree with Ron Paul on almost every issue that I've heard him talk about. And I really had a V-8 Moment when I heard Ron Paul, I did. By gosh he's so right. Why didn't I think of that, when he said I would abolish the IRS and the Federal income tax, and replace them with... NOTHING!

Because if the Federal Government and Congress stayed within their proper parameters, they wouldn't need all this money to pay for all of their corruption. **We're literally paying for our own demise.** We need to stop funding the criminal who is coming after us.

• Sheriffs?... Will you stand against tyranny?

One thing I wanted to say about the book, is that every citizen should read it. Because your Employee needs to know about it. And your Employee, that we're talking about, is your Sheriff, and anybody else needs to know about it. The Deputies too.

When you get this book, you should always get at least 1 or 2 extra copies. Keep one for yourself, and give one to your favorite deputy, or your uncle who's a police officer, or to your Sheriff. And make sure he understands what you and your neighbors really want him to do.

It all boils down to this, Sheriff, will you stand against tyranny? Can you imagine any Sheriff saying, No? *"Tyranny is not my job? Studying against tyranny is not my job."*

How bad do you think things have to get in this country before your Sheriff says, "enough is enough"?

The Monster's knocking on the door. The Monster of Despotism and Tyranny are destroying our country, and if there was ever a time in our country's history when we should be standing against tyranny, it's now.

Sheriff's, I'm asking you, will you do it? If you don't, the fate of our country is in that decision. If you understand and fight against tyranny, we win. Your citizens are protected and America continues. If you don't, America dies.

http://www.sheriffmack.com/

NO INTIMIDATION!

2
IRS and RICO
What do they have in common?

The "INTERNAL REVENUE SERVICE" is a privately owned corporation that is no part of the United States Federal Government.

The IRS draws its entire legitimate authority through the United States Revenue Code Title 26 that is not listed as positive law, in the federal register, to conduct business in the United States of America.

The United States Constitution is "bifurcated" — separated into two parts — the **internal** Federal government, and the **external** National government.

(1) The **internal** Federal government is Washington, D.C. [District of Columbia], with its 10 square mile area, and its forts and arsenals, and territories of the Virgin Islands, Samoa, and with its Secretary of the Treasury registered in Guam.

(2) The **external** National government consists of the 50 sovereign united States of America that form the Union Republic

Fact 1 - THE UNITED STATES OF AMERICA is not a country! It's a corporation ... incorporated under international law under the aegis of the crown of Great Britain!

A corporation cannot operate as a country under a corporate structure, functioning under "articles of incorporation."

The "Internal Revenue Service (IRS)" is not positioned to issue a valid assessment for any lien, levy, or seizure of property, under any legality whatsoever.

The Commissioner of Internal Revenue states openly that the American people must comply (apply) for their service voluntarily.

A classic example of this is the income-tax Form 1040 sent out that is specifically addressed as "voluntary compliance" — meaning, "voluntarily applied for."

Only a "Peace-Officer" has the executive authority to serve a judicial warrant (to a person), and then only under a court order. This is confirmed by the United States Supreme Court. IRS agents are not "law enforcement" officers.

There is no provision in the "Internal Revenue Code (IRC)" that makes anyone liable for direct taxes on income, and certainly not for filing a "1040 tax form".

Note the difference between the words, "taxpayer" and "tax payer".

The term "taxpayer" (not the two words, "tax payer") is defined in the IRC **Title 26 § 7701(a)(14)** as **any "person"** (human person, or legally created person) **"subject" to any internal revenue tax.**

The federal revenue laws apply only to "taxpayers", whereas a "tax payer" is *anybody* who has paid a tax.

There are more "non-taxpayers" in the 50 sovereign States of the Union than there are in the **internal** Federal government.

There is no such thing as an **external** National income tax.

Fact 2 — IRC **Title 26 § 1461** (civil and criminal penalties) impose liability *only upon the violation of any regulations imposed by the "Secretary",* meaning the Secretary of the Treasury that is registered in Guam. The head of administration was Manual Diaz Saldano, P.O. Box 4515, San Jean, Puerto Rico 00902.

Under "Rico Law", Criminal Conspiracy is defined as *"an organization's scheme to expand an ideology by illegal means such as violence, arson, or **intimidation**, to damage a business or property."*

Violation of which can result in organization members being sentenced to 20 years in prison, for their criminal enterprise.

Hope Deferred

Negative Averment

"I have not been presented with any material evidence that you have a claim against me through a warrant or "probable cause" through a court order by the Secretary of the Treasury, and I believe that no such evidence exists. Failure to present such material evidence within the next 21 days will be taken as aggreement."

Hope Deferred

Confirmation

Hope Deferred

Sheriffs Rise Up Against Feds

As more people became dissatisfied with federal government controls and land grabs, it was inevitable that local law enforcement would eventually see the bigger picture. At the northern California fairgrounds of Yreka last money, seven California sheriffs and another from Oregon gathered with a large group of citizens to say that they are finally going to do something about it.

"A giant has been awakened," said Plumas County, Calif. Sheriff Greg Hagwood, "and they didn't count on that," speaking of the federal bureaucracy.

With exposure of the Emergency Management Center in San Luis Obispo a few decades ago, California began to offer the rest of the nation some evidence of the psychological conditioning aimed from the federal level at state, county and city law enforcement.

Dean Wilson, sheriff of Del Norte County (Sacramento), is a great example of this great awakening. He received the loudest and longest applause for his candor in confessing past faults after apologizing for not understanding the central government assault and land grab being committed against the people, and what he should have been doing about it. Only in the past year has he done a turnaround and begun to behave as a county sheriff instead of an extension of federal law enforcement.

"I had spent a good part of my life enforcing the penal code, but not understanding my oath of office," he told the audience. "I was ignorant and naive, but now I know of the assault against our people by the federal government."

Host sheriff John Lopey of Siskiyou County, speaking about the federal environmental intervention, said: "I have told federal and state officials over and over that, yes, we want to preserve the environment, but you care more about the fish, frogs, trees and birds than you do about the human race. When will you start to balance your decisions to the needs of the people?" Later he told the audience, "We are right now in a fight for our survival."

Glenn Palmer, sheriff of Grant County, Oregon, said, "If an elected official has not taken an oath of office, he does not belong in office."

Most readers are familiar with the work of former Arizona Sheriff Richard Mack, who has spent the latter half of his life teaching sheriffs that they are the top law enforcement officers in their counties despite continuing federal intervention attempts. The ears that were deaf for so long may finally be starting to hear.

"It's becoming a national movement now," Mack told us, citing Immigration and Naturalization Service failure at the Mexican borders, the phony drug war, plus IRS and other unconstitutional intervention within these states.

His plans to take this movement national will be launched at a January meeting, where he anticipates 200 sheriffs will be in attendance.

"The county sheriff is the last line of defense guarding our people's liberty," he said.

Retired USAF Col. Richard Niemela of Reston, Va. has been exposing the federal monster for years.

He told us: "It's the surreptitious domination by international globalists insidiously using unauthorized and illegal tactics to render null and void those historic and unique powers of the sheriff."

Hope Deferred

County Sheriffs: Our First Line of Defense Against NWO

It was no surprise to us when we read an editorial in *The Washington Post* that called for the abolition of the elected sheriff's office in suburban Washington's Loudoun Country, Va. and replacing it with an unelected police force.

The statist who penned the editorial attack wrote: "A sheriff's office led by an elected sheriff may work suitably for smaller and sleepier places. It's problematic in bigger and more complex jurisdictions, where there's a need for highly skilled, professional law enforcement management free from the encumbrances of political campaigns, donors, and influence. . .

"Until now, county officials have balked at the idea of establishing a police department with an appointed chief, citing the cost of conversion. But as the county continues to grow, it needs to reconsider whether its law enforcement leadership has kept up with the times. Loudoun, with a third of a million people, the highest median income of any U.S. county, and fast-growing minority communities, is ready for a change."

Forty-eight of the 50 states have sheriff's offices. Alaska and Connecticut do not. Alaska has no counties, and Connecticut has counties but no county government. Fairfax Country is the most populous county in the Commonwealth of Virginia, with a population of 1,081,725. The popularly elected county sheriff's office runs the county jail, secures the courthouses and serves civil process. No more, no less.

However, it is the unelected Fairfax Country Police Department with a force of 1,402 that is the primary law enforcement body.

The sheriff's office has a legendary history dating back to King Nebuchadnezzar of Babylon in 600 B.C. But the present history of the sheriff's office actually dates to Saxon England during the reign of King Alfred the Great in A.D. 871, who, in order to strengthen his power and build unity in his kingdom, created the geographic district called "shire," the forerunner of the "county."

The head of each of these shires was called the "shire's reeve," who was responsible for maintaining law and order in the area. His title evolved into "shire-reef" and finally sheriff. He was the chief officer of the king, with the power of making arrests, collecting taxes, raising armies, judging lawbreakers, and jailing the guilty.

Most of us have heard of Robin Hood, the colorful hero who stole from the rich and gave his loot to the poor. Legend has it that he kept the Sheriff of Nottingham quite busy. But it was the sheriff's duty to capture outlaws such as Robin Hood, either to ensure the safety of the trade routes through Sherwood Forest or to keep them from poaching the King's deer.

In 1066 at the Battle of Hastings, Harold was defeated,

the King's power was centralized, and the sheriffs became the chief enforcers for William of Normandy.

When settlers came to Virginia they brought the concept of shire and sheriff with them. In 1634 the territory was divided into eight shires (later redesignated as counties), each with a sheriff.

President Thomas Jefferson in his *Value of Constitutions* wrote that, "The office of sheriff is the most important of all executive offices in the country [America]."

Is it time to change? No!

According to the explanations in this book, many sheriffs are waking up and realizing that they are the true law of the land!

Hope Deferred

Appendix

Hope Deferred

What Revolution Looks Like
by Chris Hedges

Welcome to the revolution. Our elites have exposed their hand. They have nothing to offer. They can destroy but they cannot build. They can repress but they cannot lead. They can steal but they cannot share. They can talk but they cannot speak.

They are as dead and useless to us as the water-soaked books, tents, sleeping bags, suitcases, food boxes and clothes that were tossed by sanitation workers Tuesday morning, 11/15/11, into garbage trucks in New York City. They have no ideas, no plans and no vision for the future.

Our decaying corporate regime has strutted in Portland, Oakland, New York and in other places, with their baton-wielding cops into a fool's paradise.

They think they can clean up "the mess" — always employing the language of personal hygiene and public security — by making us disappear.

They think we will all go home and accept their corporate nation, a nation where crime and government policy have become indistinguishable, where nothing in America, including the ordinary citizen, is deemed by those in power worth protecting or preserving, where corporate oligarchs awash in hundreds of millions of dollars are permitted to loot and pillage the last shreds of collective wealth, human capital and natural resources, a nation where the poor do not eat and workers do not work, a nation where the sick die and children go hungry, a nation where the consent of the governed and the voice of the people is a cruel joke.

Get back into your cages, they are telling us. Return to watching the lies, absurdities, trivia and celebrity gossip we feed you in 24-hour cycles on television. Invest your emotional energy in the vast system of popular entertainment. Run up your credit card debt. Pay your loans. Be thankful for the scraps we toss.

Chant back to us our phrases about democracy, greatness and freedom. Vote in our rigged political theater. Send your young men and women to fight and die in useless, unwinnable wars that provide corporations with huge profits. Stand by mutely as our bipartisan congressional supercommittee, either through consensus or cynical dysfunction, plunges you into a society without basic social services including unemployment benefits. Pay for the crimes of Wall Street.

The rogues' gallery of Wall Street crooks, such as Lloyd Blankfein at Goldman Sachs, Howard Milstein at New York Private Bank & Trust, the media tycoon Rupert Murdoch, the Koch brothers and Jamie Dimon at JPMorgan Chase & Co., no doubt think it's over.

They think it is back to the business of harvesting what is left of America to swell their personal and corporate fortunes. But they no longer have any concept of what is happening around them. They are as mystified and clueless about these uprisings as the courtiers at Versailles or in the Forbidden City who never understood until the very end that their world was collapsing.

The billionaire mayor of New York, enriched by a deregulated Wall Street, is unable to grasp why people would spend two months sleeping in an open park and marching against banks. He says he understands that the Occupy protests are "cathartic" and "entertaining," as if demonstrating against the pain of being homeless and unemployed is a form of therapy or diversion, but that it is time to let the adults handle the affairs of state. Democratic and Republican mayors, along with their parties, have sold us out. But for them this is the beginning of the end.

The historian Crane Brinton in his book "Anatomy of a Revolution" laid out the common route to revolution. The preconditions for successful revolution, Brinton argued, are discontent that affects nearly all social classes, widespread feelings of entrapment and despair, unfulfilled expectations, a unified solidarity in opposition to a tiny power elite, a refusal by scholars and thinkers to continue to defend the actions of the ruling class, an inability of government to respond to the basic needs of citizens, a steady loss of will within the power elite itself and defections from the inner circle, a crippling isolation that leaves the power elite without any allies or outside support and, finally, a financial crisis.

Our corporate elite, as far as Brinton was concerned, has amply fulfilled these preconditions. But it is Brinton's next observation that is most worth remembering.

Revolutions always begin, he wrote, by making impossible demands, that if the government met, would mean the end of the old configurations of power. The second stage, the one we have entered now, is the unsuccessful attempt by the power elite to quell the unrest and discontent through physical acts of repression.

I have seen my share of revolts, insurgencies and revolutions, from the guerrilla conflicts in the 1980s in Central America to the civil wars in Algeria, the Sudan and Yemen, to the Palestinian uprising to the revolutions in East Germany, Czechoslovakia and Romania as well as the wars in the former Yugoslavia.

George Orwell wrote that all tyrannies rule through fraud and force, but that once the fraud is exposed they must rely exclusively on force. We have now entered the era of naked force. The vast million-person bureaucracy of the internal security and surveillance state will not be used to stop terrorism, but to try and stop us.

Despotic regimes in the end collapse internally. Once the foot soldiers who are ordered to carry out acts of repression, such as the clearing of parks or arresting or even shooting demonstrators, no longer obey orders, the old regime swiftly crumbles. When the aging East German dictator Erich Honecker was unable to get paratroopers to fire on protesting crowds in Leipzig, the regime was finished.

The same refusal to employ violence doomed the communist governments in Prague and Bucharest. I watched in December 1989 as the army general that the dictator Nicolae Ceausescu had depended on to crush protests condemned him to death on Christmas Day. Tunisia's Ben Ali and Egypt's Hosni Mubarak lost power once they could no longer count on the security forces to fire into crowds.

The process of defection among the ruling class and security forces is slow and often imperceptible. These defections are advanced through a rigid adherence to nonviolence, a refusal to respond to police provocation, and a verbal respect for the blue-uniformed police — no matter how awful they can be while wading into a crowd and using batons as battering rams against human bodies.

The resignations of Oakland Mayor Jean Quan's deputy, Sharon Cornu, and the mayor's legal adviser and longtime friend, Dan Siegel, in protest over the clearing of the Oakland encampment are some of the first cracks in the edifice. "Support Occupy Oakland, not the 1% and its government facilitators," Siegel tweeted after his resignation.

There were times when I entered the ring as a boxer and knew, as did the spectators, that I was woefully mismatched. Ringers, experienced boxers in need of a tuneup or a little practice, would go to the clubs where semi-pros fought, lie about their long professional fight records, and toy with us. Those fights became about something other than winning. They became about dignity and self-respect. You fought to say something about who you were as a human being. These bouts were punishing, physically brutal and demoralizing. You would get knocked down and stagger back up. You would reel backward from a blow that felt like a cement block. You would taste the saltiness of your blood on your lips. Your vision would blur. Your ribs, the back of your neck and your abdomen would ache. Your legs would feel like lead.

But the longer you held on, the more the crowd in the club turned in your favor. No one, even you, thought you could win. But then, every once in a while, the ringer would get overconfident. He would get careless. He would become a victim of his own hubris. And you would find deep within yourself some new burst of energy, some untapped strength and, with the fury of the dispossessed, bring him down.

I have not put on a pair of boxing gloves for 30 years. But I felt this twinge of euphoria again in my stomach this morning, this utter certainty that the impossible is possible, this realization that the mighty will fall.

Is the Rothschild banking monopoly about to be dismantled?

by Benjamin Fulford, 11-01-11

The situation in Europe is making it clear to all but the most brainwashed that something historical is taking place. What is happening is that the criminal element at the very top of the Western power structure, especially at the very top of the financial system, has been cut off from their money printing machine.

As a result, the IMF and the major European and US money center banks are insolvent. No amount of lying or paper shuffling or propaganda is going to hide this fundamental truth.

The governments of Greece, Ireland, Portugal, Italy etc. know that the debts they supposedly owe to bankers were created through fraudulent book entries and thus do not have to be repaid. That is why the banks suddenly announced that Greece only had to pay back 50% of their debt even though such a write off would destroy the banks.

They are hoping for a tax payer bail-out that is just not going to happen. It is game over. The Rothschild banking nightmare is ending. Even the highly brainwashed priesthood known as Western financial gurus and journalists are starting to realize that something is not right.

The big announcement by European governments of a "solution" to the Greek and Euro crises is a case in point. If you analyze the announcement you realize that essentially the banks and governments are saying the banks will pay for 50% of the Greek debt with money they do not have.

The governments say they will pay for it by "leveraging" the money they already have. They do not say who is going to be dumb enough to finance a bankrupt gambler who wants to quadruple his risk.

Please note that as soon as the "solution" to the crisis was announced, high level begging missions were sent to Asia, including French President Sarkozy. Why would they need to go to Asia to ask for money if they had come up with a solution?

The IMF, supposedly the world's "lender of last resort" is also continuing to admit they have no money. The reason is that the IMF itself cannot prove that its money comes from legitimate sources.

The fact of the matter is that the criminal part of the world's financial system is falling apart. The IMF will soon cease to be solvent. The same is true of the World Bank. The BIS is also in trouble. In fact, the entire Rothschild banking monopoly is in deep trouble.

The freeze of "trading platforms" remains in place, meaning that the controllers of the fiat system can no longer pump new money into the system. The best they can do is reshuffle money that is already in the system. New money will only start entering the global financial system once the new asset-backed system is in place.

"The IMF and the World Bank existed to force the Rothschild banking system on the countries of the world," is how an extremely senior Chinese official explained the situation. *"Our goal is to reboot the system, to start over and set all the parameters in a fair way so that all countries benefit from the pooled assets of the people of the world and not just Europe and North America,"* he continued.

The original system was meant to have been run by the Swiss and protected by the Americans, he continued. *"The basic failure was that the system of checks and balances failed and the people who were supposed to protect the system ended up abusing it,"* he added.

What is now going to happen is that the 100 countries that have so far joined the new system, started in Monaco in August, are going to implement the new system in four stages, according to a White Dragon Society source. The US military and agencies will be involved in this process right from the beginning, he added. Efforts to intimidate generals by using corrupt institutions like the IRS to try to repossess their homes will backfire and lead to criminal prosecutions.

The first step will be a lawsuit that will be filed before November 15th against the individuals and groups who abused the Federal Reserve Board system. This will lead to liens being placed against many of the largest financial institutions in the world, according to the filers. There will also be mass arrests.

The other steps have yet to be disclosed. However, some basic truths are already known.

First of all, all honest businessmen and bankers worldwide will have nothing to worry about.

Second of all, the money created through derivatives fraud will be eliminated from the books, even if that means bankrupting many of the big Western financial institutions.

Third, major historical financial injustices will be addressed and stolen monies and assets will be returned to their rightful owners.

This will be good news for the vast majority of Western citizens as well as the inhabitants of long exploited regions like Africa.

The international banking and payment settlements systems will remain in place after the reboot. This will mean the minimum possible disruption to legitimate business.

However — as mentioned earlier — the international institutions set up and controlled by a small group of Western oligarchs after World War II will be totally revamped.

The Cabalists Struggle In Vain
by Benjamin Fulford, 11-15-11

"The cabalists struggle in vain to stop the new financial system… The global human awakening will not be stopped"

Despite seeming bad news on several fronts last week, insiders assure us that plans for a new financial system are going ahead on all fronts. Instead of perpetual war and genocide on behalf of an inbred elite, the people of the planet are choosing to end poverty, stop environmental destruction and push for a new life-centered scientific and technical revolution.

Major assistance emerged as a 59-nation group claiming to represent the Red Dragon Society or Maiona, offered its support to the new system. The Red Dragon is headed by Admiral Heemi Hau, Paramount Chief of the NGAPUHI in New Zealand and links 59 countries plus 2700 tribes mostly in the South Pacific Region. They back their words with treaties with the British Empire going back to the 1700's as well as older treaties going back to 804 CE. ("Common Era")

This is yet another step in the unstoppable global awakening that will forever take control of the planet out of the hands of the gangsters who have been terrifying us for so long.

Here is a part of what the Maiona group proposes:

Our objective is to overcome scarcity and provide for the needs of all the world's people through the creation of a sustainable, living, vibrant civilization that will eliminate all wars, fears, poverty and hunger.

Resources will be assessed globally that we may cover the needs of the total populations requirement for housing, food, water, health, transport, education and recreation, and will also be co-ordinated in with the needs of other species that make up the web of life on the planet.

Sources of energy will be explored and developed, but not be limited to, wind, ocean tides, currents, temperature differentials, falling water, geothermal, electrostatic, hydrogen, algae, biomass, gravity, bacteria, phase transformation, thermionics, magnification and fusion energy.

Cities can be constructed circular, linear, underground, floating or underwater, but will all be built utilizing better resource and construction techniques. These cities would all have the ability to supply their own nutritional requirements, giving independence and sustainability.

Geometrically elegant arrangements, parks, gardens, reefs all designed to operate with efficient uses of energy and resource that co-exist with their natural surroundings. Design and development must work in with the environment providing clean air, water, food, health, nutrition, entertainment, accessibility, care and education.

That is the sort of thinking that the gangsters who took over the global financial system have proven themselves to be incapable of. They talk instead of never ending "wars on terror," and "homeland security," and "threat levels," while pouring all of the planets free resources either into a massive military-industrial murder machine or a decadent lifestyle for a tiny elite.

These gangsters, for their part, made a big push last week in an effort to make it seem they were still in charge. In Europe they placed cabal flunkies in power in Greece and Italy after threatening the previous democratically elected leaders into resigning. This show of force, however, is still not backed by any show of money. The Rotschild/Rockefeller cabalists remain bankrupt and any attempts at asserting control in Europe will fail. In fact, the Greeks have contacted the White Dragon Society to inform them they will pretend to go along with the cabalists in order to get a new hit of paper money but that when the time comes to pay back, they will, as the Irish have done, demand proof that he bankers had a legal right to lend that "money," in the first place.

In Japan as well, there were signs that all was not well. J. Rockefeller, one of the masterminds of the Tsunami, earthquake and nuclear attacks against Japan was spotted making a tour of the disaster zone and promising "assistance." At the same time, the monster-toad Henry Kissinger was paraded on Japanese TV on November 11th, talking to Japanese Prime Minister Yoshihiko Noda. However, Noda lived up to his name, which means "does not give," in Spanish and Kissinger and Rockefeller left Japan empty handed.

Ingratitude, Disdain   65

IMF Director Christine Lagarde also returned empty-handed from her week long begging tour of Russia, China and Japan. She no doubt had it explained to her that the 1.1 billion people who did not have enough food to eat were a greater priority than underfunded pensions for prematurely retired Europeans.

While here, Kissinger also tried to hire gangsters to kill this writer but found no takers, according to Japanese underground sources. Now that his fraudulent mirror account trading platforms have been shut down it would seem his funny money is no longer accepted by the underworld here.

In other news, an informant approached this writer last week with new details about the 1995 incident in which the Aum Shinrikyo sect released poison gas in the Tokyo subway system. The informant claims she was kidnapped, drugged, raped and tortured into becoming a MK-ultra type agent for North Korean gangsters.

She said the North Koreans were taking orders from Jewish Al-Qaeda type agents. The entire subway incident was engineered to "terrorize the Japanese," she claims. The informant provided this writer with specific names and contact information for the gangsters involved. According to her and other sources, these same gangsters had foreknowledge of the March 11, 2011 tsunami, earthquake and nuclear attacks on Japan.

The White Dragon Society is contacting these gangsters to try to see if they will be willing to testify about 311 and the Aum incident in exchange for immunity.

Needless to say the Japanese security police have also been informed.

However, according to sources among both the yakuza and Japanese military intelligence, senior members of the Japanese police forces have also been working for the cabal and have been bribed and blackmailed in the past so it is unlikely we will see any official police action on 311 just yet.

Nonetheless, the Japanese police/military/gangster nexus is now refusing to accept new assignments from the cabalists. Most are sitting on the fence and waiting to see how the battle for control of the global financial system turns out.

On that front, the only thing that is certain is that the old system is mathematically doomed. The criminal cabal in Wall Street, the Vatican, Washington D.C. and the London "City" financial district know their time is up but they remain arrogant, stubborn and dangerous.

Nonetheless, over 107 countries have agreed to the new financial system discussed in Monaco in August. In addition, the 59-nation Red Dragon group is also working with the White Dragon. That means at least 166 nations now support the new system. The global human awakening will not be stopped.

Hope Deferred

"Mortals try in vain to slay Truth with the steel or the stake, but error falls only before the sword of Spirit."

M.B.E.

Hope Deferred

Other Publications

NESARA: National *Economic Security and Reformation Act*
http://tinyurl.com/c8u42q6

History of Banking: *An Asian Perspective*
http://tinyurl.com/boeehjl

The People's Voice: *Former Arizona Sheriff Richard Mack*
http://tinyurl.com/d62fyg3

Asset Protection: *Pure Trust Organizations*
http://tinyurl.com/btrjfqp

The Matrix As It Is: *A Different Point Of View*
http://tinyurl.com/ckrbkge

From Debt To Prosperity: *'Social Credit' Defined*
http://tinyurl.com/d2tjmw3

Give Yourself Credit: *Money Doesn't Grow On Trees*
http://tinyurl.com/d7tphuv

My Home Is My Castle: *Beware Of The Dog*
http://tinyurl.com/bmzxc2n

Commercial Redemption: *The Hidden Truth*
http://tinyurl.com/d9etg7w

Hardcore Redemption-In-Law: *Commercial Freedom And Release*
http://tinyurl.com/cl65vrz

Oil Beneath Our Feet: *America's Energy Non-Crisis*
http://tinyurl.com/btlzqxf

Hope Deferred

Untold History Of America: *Let The Truth Be Told*
http://tinyurl.com/bu9kjjc

Debtocracy: *& Odious Debt Explained*
http://tinyurl.com/cooqzuz

New Beginning Study Course: *Connect The Dots And See*
http://tinyurl.com/cxpk42p

Monitions of a Mountain Man: *Manna, Money, & Me*
http://tinyurl.com/cusgcqs

Maine Street Miracle: *Saving Yourself And America*
http://tinyurl.com/d4yktlw

Reclaim Your Sovereignty: *Take Back Your Christian Name*
http://tinyurl.com/cf5taxh

Gun Carry In The USA: Your Right To Self-defence
http://tinyurl.com/cdn3y3y

Climategate Debunked: *Big Brother, Main Stream Media*
http://tinyurl.com/d6gy2xz

Epistle to the Americans I: *What you don't
know about The Income Tax*
http://tinyurl.com/d99ujzm

Epistle to the Americans II: *What you don't
know about American History*
http://tinyurl.com/cnyghyz

Epistle to the Americans III: *What you don't
know about Money*
http://tinyurl.com/cp8nrh8